100 Thoughts

Lee Barmak

ISBN: 0615977901
ISBN-13:9780615977904

.

I will not protest if someone corrects me on any of the perspective based thoughts from 2013-2014. I will not say that I am the originator of all thoughts written on these pages since many similar sayings have been spoken by man long before my time.

A MAN WITHOUT WORK DIES
PREMATURELY. A MAN WHO HATES
HIS WORK IS ALREADY DEAD.

HE WHO HAS NOT EXPERIENCED
PAIN, IS NOT WHO YOU WANT ON
YOUR SIDE IN A FIGHT.

ALWAYS GO DIRECTLY TO THE
SOURCE OF THE PROBLEM. TO DO
OTHERWISE IS TO SHOW LACK OF
CHARACTER. IN THIS AGE, WE
ATTACK SYMPTOMS INSTEAD OF
PROBLEMS.

Lee Barmak

MAN, WHO IS LAZY TO SPIT
SEEDS FROM WATERMELON AND
WAITS FOR A WATERMELON
WITHOUT SEEDS, IS A MAN WHO
ISN'T JUST LAZY, BUT SPOILED.

BEFORE STARTING A SERIOUS
WORKOUT AND DIET ROUTINE,
PLACE SOME CHIPS AND
CHOCOLATE IN THE OPEN. IF YOU
SUCCUMB TO THE TEMPTATION,
YOUR CONVICTION AND
MOTIVATION IS WEAK. AVERAGE
IS PLENTIFUL, GREAT IS IN
DEMAND.

FAKE COLD HUGS ARE TOO COMMON
NOW A DAYS.

WHEN IN A CORNER, DON'T FALL ON YOUR KNEES, FIGHT. IF DEATH IS CERTAIN, FIGHT HARDER.

QUITTING ON YOURSELF IS
QUITTING ON THE WORLD. THE
WORLD NEEDS PEOPLE WHO KNOW
WHAT IT'S LIKE TO HIT ROCK
BOTTOM AND REBOUND.

NEVER REWARD A MAN WHO ISN'T
TRYING. NEVER GIVE A CHILD A
TROPHY FOR NOT WINNING.

HOW ARE YOU TO CHANGE THE WORLD IF YOU FORGET TO TIE YOUR SHOES?

BUT SIR, HOW ARE YOU TO
MOVE FORWARD WITHOUT A
WRITTEN PLAN?

HOW CAN MAN FORGET WHO HE
IS IF HE NEVER DISCOVERED
WHO HE WAS?

HE WHO BLAMES THE RICH
MAN WILL NEVER BE RICH,
FOR HE WILL ALWAYS HAVE
THE RICH MAN TO BLAME FOR
HIS MISFORTUNES.

10Lee Barmak

TO HIDE BEHIND THE BACK
OF YOUR COMRADE IS WORSE
THAN TO SHOOT YOUR
COMRADE IN THE BACK.

MANKIND. A CURE AND A
DISEASE PACKAGED TOGETHER
AND SET FREE ON THE
COSMOS.

IF PEOPLE DON'T LOOK UP
TO YOU, THEN HOW DO THEY
LOOK AT YOU?

STICKING TO EXTREMES FOR A
LONG TIME WILL CAUSE A
BURNOUT. NOT STICKING TO
EXTREMES AT DESPERATE TIMES
IS MORE DANGEROUS THAN A
BURNOUT.

A SMALL ANIMAL THAT CAN
BITE A BIG ANIMAL AND GET
AWAY ON A CONSISTENT
BASIS MAKES THE SMALL
ANIMAL THE ALPHA. NOT
EVERYONE IS BORN A TIGER,
BUT EVERYONE IS BORN.

IF IT'S NOT FRUITFUL,
NEED NOT SPEND TIME ON
THE TASK. BUT IF THAT WAS
THE CASE, TELEVISION
STATIONS WOULD BE OUT OF
BUSINESS.

TRUE SPIRIT OF A POOR MAN
IS REVEALED EVERY BLACK
FRIDAY.

FEAR SOMETIMES IS THE
ONLYTHING THAT KEEPS THE
WICKED CHECKED. SUFFOCATION
OF EVIL BY FEAR IS AN EVIL IN
ITSELF THAT AT TIMES NEEDS TO
BE ENDURED.

GUESTS WHO DO NOT OFFER TO
PAY FOR GAS, FOOD, AND OTHER
MISCELLANEOUS EXPENSES ARE
NOT GUESTS. THEY ARE BURDENS.
HE, WHO DOES NOT OFFER, IS
SELFISH AND OR POORLY
CULTURED AND NEEDS A WAKEUP
CALL. IF YOU ALLOW THESE
PEOPLE TO RIDE YOU, ONLY YOU
ARE TO BLAME.

WHEN LIFE NO LONGER FEELS
EXCITING, WHEN MONOTONOUS
AUTOPILOT ALLOWS YOU TO
EXPERIENCE NOTHING BUT AN
EXCITEMENT FREE ROAD,
RETHINK YOUR LIFE. THIS
ROAD, IF UNCHANGED LEADS
TO DEPRESSION. DEPRESSION
TO DESPERATION.

THE ONE THING HOLDING THE
WORLD BACK FROM COMPLETE
TRANSFORMATION,AND WEALTH
OF UNCHARTED LEVELS FOR
ALL PEOPLE, IS
CORRUPTION.

PATRIOTS OF THE WORLD FOR
JUST HUMAN UNIFICATION
AND ECOLOGICAL
REVOLUTION, WHERE ARE
YOU?

IN A COUNTRY WHERE PEOPLE'S
PSYCHOLOGY IS OPEN,
CORRUPTION IS A MAJOR PROBLEM
AND YET THE PEOPLE ARE HAPPY.
IN A COUNTRY WHERE PEOPLE'S
PSYCHOLOGY IS CLOSED,
STRUCTURE, ORDER AND LAW ARE
PREDOMINANT SOCIAL ELEMENTS.
UNFORTUNATLEY THE PEOPLE
SUFFER WITHIN.

HOW ARE WE TO BUILD A BETTER
WORLD IF MANS LOYALTY IS
FIRST TO HIS PERSPECTIVE?

U.G.C.M.
United Global
Commonwealth Of Man.

A MANS WORD SHOULD CARRY
MORE WEIGHT THAN A
CONTRACT SIGNED IN BLOOD.
THE WORLD OF TODAY HAS
FORGOTTEN, OR PERHAPS
JUST NEVER KNEW WHAT IT
MEANS TO GIVE A WORD AND
GIVE UP ALL FOR THAT WORD
IF NEED BE.

TORTURE A MAN LONG ENOUGH AND
ONE PLUS ONE WILL NOT EQUAL
TWO. IT WILL EQUAL WHATEVER
YOU TELL HIM IT EQUALS.

CLOTHING, FEEDING AND
EDUCATING A CHILD IS
POINTLESS IF THE CHILD DOES
NOT BELIEVE THAT HE CAN.

JUST BECAUSE A MAN LOOKS LIKE
A GOD ON THE OUTSIDE, DOES
NOT MEAN THAT HE ISN'T BROKEN
ON THE INSIDE.

IN CONVERSATION, WHEN THE
OTHER PARTY STARTS TO GIVE
INFORMATION AND EXPLANATIONS
ABOUT CERTAIN ACTIONS WHEN
YOU DID NOT ASK FOR THEM, IT
SIGNIFIES THAT THE PARTY IS
GUILTY, FEARFUL OR UNSURE AS
TO HOW YOUR PERCEPTION OF
THEM IS FORMING.

Lee Barmak

NEVER GO TO WAR UNLESS YOU
ARE READY TO GIVE UP
EVERYTHING FOR THE CAUSE THAT
THE FIGHT IS FOUGHT FOR.
NEVER GO TO WAR FOR A MAN WHO
WILL NOT GIVE UP HIS LIFE TO
WIN THE WAR.

IF YOU CARE FOR YOUR LEADER
BE SURE TO TEST HIM. HE MAY
NOT LIKE YOU, BUT A PROVEN
LEADER OFF THE BATTELFIELD IN
TIME OF CALM IS BETTER READY
FOR CHALLENGES AHEAD.

AS LONG AS THE WRONG MEN HAVE
GUNS IN AFRICA, AFRICA WILL
EXIST IN A STATE POVERTY AND
ATROCITY. THE UN HAS FAILED.
UNLESS ANOTHER FORCE
BULLDOZES THE VIOLENCE WITH A
JUST TREMBLING BLOW AND
ESTABLISHES A PERMANENT
BALANCED SYSTEM OF
GOVERNMENT,-CHILDREN, WOMEN
AND MEN WHO ARE INNOCENT WILL
CONTINUE TO PARISH AND SCREAM
IN HORROR While the Western
world awaits in anticipation
for the next television show
to reveal if Monica really
meant what she said.

HE WHO FEARS TO ACT, IS
DESTINED FOR A LIFE OF
MEDIOCRACY.

BLINDLY STARING AT A
SMARTPHONE. A PORTRAIT OF A
GENERATION. STORMING THE
BEACHES OF NORMANDY OR
HOLDING STALINGRAD IS NOT FOR
YOU. BESIDES, HOW WOULD YOU
KNOW WHAT HAPPENED THERE
WITHOUT YOUR SMART PHONE?

TO BE OFFENDED BY A FOOL OR A
MAN OF IGNORANCE IS TO BE A
FOOL OR A MAN OF IGNORANCE.
DEFEND PRINCIPALS, CARE NOT
FOR EMPTY WORDS OF IGNORANT
MEN.

CHEAPNESS IS A TRAIT OF
SELFISHNESS. FRUGALITY IS A
TRAIT OF WISDOM.

To do an act of kindness and not to speak of it to others is to truly do an act of good. For the second we share our good actions we elevate our own self-worth in the eyes of others. If the act is truly for the sake of another and not oneself, it is not spoken of. To speak or promote the act is to seem as a good (man/woman) while wearing an invisible mask of a boaster.

This generation does not
know pain, it's submerged
in laziness and it believes
itself to be entitled. In
this life, the only person
who owes you anything is
you, so don't be crying
like a victim later for
choices that you made today
and yesterday. Take
responsibility. Make
something of yourself. You
still have tomorrow.

SELF-PITY HAS NEVER
SOLVED ANYTHING

WANT TO UNDERSTAND THE
DEEPNESS OF A CULTURE? LISTEN
TO ITS MUSIC.

PEOPLE, PRIMARILY PATRIOTS
SPEAK OF FREEDOM. BUT DO THEY
REALLY KNOW WHAT FREEDOM IS
IF THEY NEVER EXPERIENCED THE
LOSS OF IT?

Lee Barmak

THE MOST IMPORTANT CLASS
MISSING IN AMERICA IS *LIFE
101.* WHAT GOOD IS A CLASSICAL
EDUCATION WHERE IT TEACHES
NOT EVEN THE MOST BASIC
PRINCIPALS OF POST SCHOOL
LIFE?

48

WHILE WE ARE STREAMING MOVIES
HERE, THE WORLD IS CRYING OUT
FOR HELP IN DESPERATION
THERE.

A TRUE FRIEND WILL GIVE HIS
KIDNEY WITHOUT ASKING WHY.

Upon the kingdom of Earth, you will encounter snakes, rats, bears, lions, foxes, rabbits, dogs and weasels. Know how to spot, deflect, aid, use, destroy and protect each one. However, just because you know how to become or do these things, does not mean you should become anything but what the situation demands you to be. Word of advice. Unless the situation completely demands it, do not become the snake or the rat.

THE PROBLEM WITH MANY
COMPANIES OF TODAY, IS THAT
THEY ARE RUN BY MANAGERS, NOT
LEADERS.

AN AMBITIOUS MAN WITH A PLAN
HAS NO NEED FOR A WINNING
LOTTERY TICKET.

IN BUSINESS AS IN SOCIAL
LIFE, IF YOU LEAVE A MESSAGE
ON THE ANSWERING MACHINE AND
DO NOT HEAR A REPLY SHORTLY,
YOU ARE NOT A PRIORITY.

A FATHERLESS KINGDOM, THE NEW
WESTERN STANDARD.

A BROKE BUSINESS PROFESSOR.
ANOTHER EDUCATED MAN WITH NO
LIFE EXPERIENCE.

A SHADOW ALWAYS FOLLOWS, LIKE
REPUTATION.

WE COULD BUILD AN EMPIRE IN
SPACE, INSTEAD WE CHOOSE
BICKERING AMONGST OURSELVES.
THANK YOU MEDIA FOR
DEGENERATING THE HUMAN
SPECIES.

ONE PROBLEM WITH HARD LINE
ATHEISTS AS WITH FANATICS IS
THAT THEY ARE TOO MUCH ALIKE.

THROUGH TIME, OUR FINITE
COMPREHENSION EDGES TOWARDS
NEW UNDERSTANDINGS.

I am still waiting to snap
out of this reality to only
realize that it was a
videogame made to seem as
every second in the real
world expanded to me as a
year in this one. Maybe In
the real world I am only
twelve and a new randomly
generated game experience is
something I go through daily
to be taught valuable
lessons. Lessons I can share
with the family at the dinner
table on a far distant planet
that no longer lives in a
world of hate, murder,
starvation and corruption.
The light at the end of the
tunnel is nothing but a
snapping of back to reality
and return of memory.

PERSPECTIVE IS REALITY, IS
LIFE, IS YOU. IN WHAT
BEGINNINGS DOES YOUR
PERSPECTIVE ORIGINATE?

NAYSAYERS, SINCE WHEN DID YOU
BECOME THE AUTHORITY ON WHAT
CAN AND CANNOT BE DONE WHEN
YOU, LACK THE VISION AND THE
DRIVE TO TRY?

SHALLOWNESS ENGULFED BY A
VICTIMS MENTALITY AND PROPPED
UP BY A SENSE OF ENTITLEMENT,
THE EMERGING AND ACCEPTED
THOUGHT PATTERN OF WESTERN
CIVILIZATION.

YESTERDAY'S WORRIES, IS AMPLIFIED STRESS TODAY, OF TROUBLES THAT MAY NOT COME TOMORROW.

THE LEFT SCREAMS AT THE RIGHT
AND THE RIGHT SCREAMS AT THE
LEFT. WE LOST BALANCE DUE TO
THIS NEVER ENDING INTERNAL
WAR. WITHOUT COMPROMISE,
NOTHING WILL CHANGE.

HUMAN TOUCH IS A WONDERFUL
THING, HOWEVER IT IS NOT TO
BE CONFUSED WITH LOVE.

WHEN ONE CHOOSES THE PATH OF
BUSINESS, IT IS MORE
IMPORTANT TO STUDY SYSTEMS
FIRST HAND TO BECOME OWNER,
THAN THE PERSUIT OF A
CLASSICAL EDUCATION TO BECOME
MANAGER.

AT WHAT POINT DID WE STOP
CALLING THINGS FOR WHAT THEY
ARE TO AVOID HURTING
SOMEONE'S FEELINGS? SINCE
WHEN DID FEELINGS BECOME MORE
IMPORTANT THAN FACTS?

Out of shape, out of mind,
out of values, out of work.
It's ok honey, it's not your
fault, it's everyone but you
who is responsible. ASK NOT
WHAT THE WORLD CAN DO FOR
YOU, BUT WHAT YOU CAN DO FOR
THE WORLD. Unfortunately you
can't do shit for the world
and much less your country if
it's not your fault.

-Thought evolved from J.F.K.

IDIOTIC PARALYSIS IS MORE
CONTAGIOUS THAN THE SPANISH
FLU.

POLITICS. THE WORST POISON
I'VE EVER TASTED AND LIVED.

WHAT BETTER PLACE TO HIDE
THAN IN THE LIGHT. WHAT
BETTER PLACE TO BE OPEN, LOUD
AND FEARLESS THAN IN THE
DARK.

Lee Barmak

ARE YOU A MAN OF FAITH OR ARE
YOU AN ATHEIST? I AM BUT A
FINITE BEING LIVING IN WHAT I
PERCEIVE TO BE AN INFINITE
UNIVERSE. MAKE OF THAT WHAT
YOU WILL.

I NEVER MET A GREAT MAN WHOSE
HANDS WERE CLEAN.

CONSTRAINTS ARE FOREVER WORN
BY THOSE WHO DO NOT STRETCH
THEIR MINDS.

FIGHTING ONESELF TO OVERCOME
ONESELF IS THE FIRST AND
HARDEST STEP OF CHANGE.

IF ALL MAJOR POLITICAL
PARTIES DID AS MUCH AS THEY
TALKED THEN WE WOULD ACTUALLY
GET SOMEWHERE.

IF THE ONE BELOW YOU CANNOT
UNDERSTAND YOU, THEN YOU
HAVEN'T REALLEY SAID
ANYTHING.

REWARD OR PUNISH, BUT NEVER
NEGLECT.

IF YOUR PEOPLE ARE NOT
TESTED, HOW DO YOU KNOW OF
THEIR TRUE LOYALTY AND
CHARACTER?

Lee Barmak

DON'T MAKE A FOREST OUT OF A
TREE.

THE BEST TANK IN THE WORLD
WILL NOT GO FAR WITHOUT FUEL
OR HIT ITS TARGET WHITHOUT A
SHELL.

A UNITED EARTH FEDERATION
WILL NOT START WITHOUT A
UNITED GLOBAL FEDERAL FRONT.

SHOW THE PEOPLE HOW TO SEE
THINGS HEAD ON. TO SHOW A
THING FROM AN ANGLE IS TO NO
LONGER PERCEIVE THAT THING AS
INTENDED.

Lee Barmak

TAKE AWAY POINTLESS ELEMENTS
OF EDUCATION AND TEACH A MAN
A TRADE FIRST. THAT WAY AFTER
HE RECEIVES HIS EDUCATION HE
STILL HAS A TRADE TO FALL
BACK ON.

A PERSON IS LIKE A PILLAR.
BUILD THE PILLAR WRONG AND IT
WILL NOT HOLD.

THERE IS MORE THAN ONE WAY TO
BUILD A STRONG PILLAR.

THE ABILITY TO BEND WHILE
UPHOLDING PRINCIPALS IS TRULY
A MASTERY OF GOOD LEADERSHIP.

QUESTIONS THAT START OFF BY
GIVING MUCH DETAIL PRIOR TO
THE ACTUAL QUESTION ARE
GEARED TO SWAY OPINION OR SET
UP THE ONE ANSWERING THE
QUESTION.

FIGHT THE FAT LION, NOT THE
STARVED WOLF.

THE DAY THE WORLD IS INVADED
IS THE DAY HUMANITY UNITES
AND PUTS ITS DIFFERENCES
ASIDE.

JUST BECAUSE YOU ARE RIGHT
DOES NOT MEAN YOU ARE RIGHT
IF YOU ARE WEAK.

EUROPE IS DONE. ITS
INDIVIDUALITY IS LOST. LONG
LIVE THE EURO.

WHEN WORLD PATRIOTISM AS A
WHOLE TAKES HOLD WE JUST
MIGHT MAKE IT.

LACK OF SWEAT IMPLIES A LACK
OF A STRESS LEVEL NECESSARY
FOR ACHIEVING DIFFICULT
GOALS.

THE SHIT YOU PULLED ME INTO
YOU CALL A SITUATION?

WHEN OTHERS SEE YOU WITH THE
ENEMY HAVING A GOOD TIME, THE
DEATH OF THAT ENEMY, WILL NOT
BEFALL SUSPICION ON TO YOU.

WHEN ONE KILLS BY ACCIDENT AS
INVADER, IT MAKES NO
DIFFERENCE. HE WILL BE HATED
ALONG WITH HIS COUNTRYMEN FOR
GENERATIONS.

THIS DOES NOT MAKE ME FEEL
GOOD. I'M TIRED...... I WONDER IF
THE MEN ON IWO JIMA SAID THE
SAME THING.

THE RIGHT WING MAN IN
BUSINESS MUST BE COMPETENT
AND ANYTHING BUT YOUR FRIEND.

Lee Barmak

MAYBE HOBBS WAS RIGHT.

.